COUNTING TO 9,999

COUNTING TO 9,999

James Kirkup

Hub Editions

James Kirkup in Hub Editions

Haiku, Haiku Sequences & Tanka

Shooting Stars
First Fireworks
Blue Bamboo
Formulas for Chaos
Utsusemi

One Line Poems

Short Takes
Noems, Poems & Koans

ISBN 1 870653 59 9

Hub Editions
4 Victoria Cottages
Church Road
Terrington St John
Wisbech Cambridgeshire
England PE9 7SS

This book of haiku is divided into the traditional seasons and is mostly in traditional form interspersed by occasional 'free form' haiku and a few tanka. And some senryu at the end.

The cover shows a certain method of counting devised in the ninth century by the Iberian theologian Rabano Mauro and is taken from a document belonging to that period. The system allows one to count up to 9,999 on the fingers of the left hand. The Japanese manner of counting, often used in the counting of haiku syllables, though much simpler, resembles this Arab mathematical method.

The 'Syllogisms after Cioran' were inspired by Emil Cioran's

SYLLOGISMES DE L'AMERTUNE

first published by Gallimard in 1952, reprinted 1980.

A fool sees not the same tree
as a wise man sees

(William Blake: The Marriage of Heaven and Hell)

SPRING

Listening to spring —
the enormous ears of two
satellite dishes

Two lovers hunched in
March gale lighting cigarettes
from a single flame

Pat-ball with paper
balloons — blowing them up with
lips I long to kiss

Strung on long bamboos
the family wash, patterned
with first plum petals

In the plum orchard
a white enamel ewer
full of rain water

Somewhere at the heart
of the dark cedar grove
wild cherry blooming

Tufts of fresh grass
growing between the stone flags
of the south terrace

On the fresh green grass
the spring clouds' flying carpets
transport our own shades

Space age balconies
of modern apartment blocks —
kimono airing

Students' spring picnic —
cutlery courtesy of
airlines of the world

On the washing line
pathetic shirts helplessly
waving empty arms

spring wind
  blowing new grass
    against tombstones

haiquotes

The first willow leaves
pale gold, that take the winds
of March with beauty

In 'the droghte of Marche'
the sunbaked mud of ricefields
is hot underfoot

Sermons in stones — and
in the webs the spiders spin
obituaries

A fool sees not the same
tree as a wise man sees — so
who's an April fool?

SUMMER

The bright green frog jumps
out of its bright green skin — then
jumps back in again

Through thick mist, patches
of flowering gorse, bright gold
among lichened rocks

Pink watermelon —
green lizard's mouth, panting in
the midsummer heat

A reclining figure,
asleep in its marble dream
of swans and fountains

The street lamp casting
moving shadows on shōji —
summer of a tree

A dancer's wide skirts
spread out in fields of flowers —
summer Mount Fuji

Open windows hang
summer dresses on passing
clothes hangers of clouds

In the summer heat
beside the tobacco kiosk
a panting bullock

The droppings of wild
horses, plug tobacco brown
on the express lane

The sunflower fields
charred black by fires in the plain —
in morning coolness

Constellations of
Queen Ann's lace upon dark green
skies of summer leaves

On the empty field
a single dandelion —
horses whinnying

Somewhere in the hills
there are hidden lakes — I sense
their reflected light

Orbiting space ships
locking into each other —
thunderclouds rising

A flash of June lightning
snatches from darkness one small
corner of the bay

AUTUMN

The apple orchards —
dark bough hung with the pale lamps
of unripe pippins

On the bird box roof
droppings are purple around
elderberry seeds

Farmhand stands looking
over his shoulder — pissing
on the cabbage patch

Immobile mobiles —
the clouds of autumn hanging
in a windless sky

Forest of girders —
September sunlight dappling
a factory floor

Once the path swept clean
it has to be swept again —
the start of autumn

Newsboy's motorbike
at 4 am — memory
of autumn mornings

Neglected garden —
chrysanthemum bushes and
faded raffia

Plastered on ‘Le Dôme’
terrace skylights, plane tree leaves
from an autumn sky

Autumn has arrived
this morning with a slug
climbing the shōji

An old bicycle
covered with spiders’ webs
in the mountain mist

Only the highway
twisting and turning into
fog in the mountains

Rainwater falling
into a metal bucket
has an autumn sound

Through the changing leaves
the plunging waters also
changing their colours

Woodcutters' bonfires
smoking in the morning mist
of recent clearings

The woodcutters' songs
echo the clang of axes
in the autumn mists

All the wagtails' white
petticoats are showing — hail
storm in September

Coming out of a tunnel
discover a lost château
in autumn sunshine
(near Souillac)

I refuse to wear
the flower of forgetting
on Remembrance Day

WINTER

From the chalet eaves,
icicles' melting daggers
dripping crystal blood

In a long shot, how
tiny the young skater at
the rink's dead centre

In a mountain's most
secret place, a stash of snow
till the hottest day

Apartment living —
to see the first ice only
now — on the bird bath

Ropes of icicles
binding the well bucket to
overhanging boughs

From a distant pass
trucks' extra loads of snow — down
through snowless valleys

In the falling snow
a white dog appears — only
the black eyes, black nose

On the ancient pond
only stepping stones covered
with the first snowfall

The bird bath water
sculpted into abstract shapes
by the winter wind

Inside a window
the evening sun has dropped — but
a new one rises
(Magritte)

New Year's day — the groan
of snow ploughs over the pass —
groaning through first dreams

On the shortest day
my shadow is pale blue on
a tomb's marble wall

The peak's first snowfall
shining through the framework of
a half-built chalet

The river is more
durable than its bridges:
shadows of dawn clouds

A hard day's skiing –
in the chalet loud snores and
smells of drying socks

Winter sunset clouds –
wild geese slowly migrating
with long outstretched necks

Snow flowers falling
in a shaft of sun between
factory chimneys

Old snows' slabs of grey
concrete shore up forever
slopes of flattened grass

The architecture
of icebergs is a mirage
of future cities

On the window panes
a sound of butterflies' wings —
the driven snowflakes

Phantom iceberg
piloted by the spectre
of a dead sea-dog

Glimpsed between the hills
of tea-plantations, Fuji's
phantom iceberg slides

On the South Terrace
patches of melting snow are
the sky's random clouds

Cold winter moon
shining all night long — shining
on the fires of Kobe

Postman with a smile
delivers our Christmas cards —
waiting for a tip

The melting mazes
of snow-streaked mountain-sides — all
entrances, exits

My kokeshi dolls
imperturbably gazing
at the falling snow

With its birds perching,
a bare tree's shadow stencilled
on the virgin snow

No other flower
in the winter garden but
the rose of Christmas
(Hellébore noir)

Christmas tree of stars —
snowflake moon
slowly melting

MICHEL NOIR
From *J'entends une fourmi*
(Listening to the Ants)
Editions de la Différence, Paris 1995
Translated by James Kirkup

Scent of lime flowers —
it lies softly weeping — my
violoncello

Senteur de tilleul.
Il pleure doucement —
Le violoncelle

The end of winter —
pale violet colour of
paulownia flowers

Dès la fin de l'hiver
Le violet pâle
Des fleurs de paulownia

MOON

Cold moonlight piercing
to the bone. In the kitchen
the eggs are stark white

New moon – hairline crack
in observatory dome –
cat's vigilant lids

Full moon shining on
the lowered shutters – but still
it pierces the cracks

What I thought was snow
was moonlight on the terrace –
already morning

Great dormitory
of life, inhabited by
dreams without meaning

Full moon shining
on a sundial –
time out

SPORTS

The ski jumper jumps
off the slope in a snowstorm
and never comes down

Old priests play better
at kemari hajime
than young novices

Flowers in water —
closing, opening, closing —
synchronised swimming

Ladylike noseclip
on the synchronised swimmer —
got to be perfect

The long-jumper shakes
sand out of his running shoes —
summer eve practice

I prefer losers
to winners — unsporting ones
to hooligan stars

But I want to see
the goalkeeper’s despair — not
the stupid triumph

Hooked on Prozac? No.
Heroin, cocaine, crack? No
— Poets are born high

In the shadow
  of the ski jump
    lovers kissing

SHADOWS

I turned round to see
if my shadow was still there:
it, too, had turned round

My shadow walking
in front of me and in step —
summer wind blowing

Butterfly shadows
tumbling on one another
in the poppy field

A speckled moth lies
in the shadow on the edge
of a whitewashed wall

Winter shadow
  in the winter sun
    pale on the wall

SUN

At Olympia
the cock's archaic crowing
in the rising sun

Winter sun gleaming
through the storm clouds, low above
the highest mountain

Through the clouds, the light
of a cooking foil sun — pale
as an omelette

A full rainbow right
over the Arc de Triomphe —
the Unknown Soldier

Sunlight from behind
a passing cloud strikes just one
roof for a second

Winter sun rising —
blood orange squeezed between dark
cloud, dark horizon
(Yasuo Kazuki)

Rippling in the wind —
a sunset in the bird bath
holding all heaven

My bright morning star
faded in the sunrise — but
it is still shining

Fresh-fallen snow —
cowbells toll clearly
before sunrise

Sunrise stains
the peaks — a piste's
pink plastic fence

BIRDS

Vast flocks of seagulls —
the waves themselves are rising
on a thousand wings

One of the strangest
of all my relationships —
love for a wagtail

Mating in the snow —
the female wagtail goes on
pecking at crumbs

Wagtail's face — a mask
by Longhi in a picture
of the carnival

Evening skies — now
departing starlings swarm thick
as swirling tea leaves

Wagtails, the colours
of our winter landscapes — grey
as the mountain rocks,
black as the forests of fir,
white as the snow's first feathers.

Swirling tea leaves
  cup of water — starlings
    in winter skies

DREAMS

Long night of bad dreams:
but at dawn, careless swallows
swim in limpid sky

A tree dreams standing —
in my dream of a forest
it dreams I am there

A dream at the end
of the night always comes true —
dream on, sad dreamer

Dreaming in the pose —
one long leg extended — of
Grisi in La Sylphide

Dreams — my kind
of sadness —
no one else's

Sleepless on
my head's heavy
pillow

Somnambulism
of the dead
deepsea diver

Plumb the
depths but with
a smile

CREATURES

A red dragonfly
perched between two prickles
on the barbed wire fence

Bluebottle flying
round the kitchen — the droning
chant of temple monks

The silk of spiders
is stronger than steel — a web
for insect prisons

A withered leaf's veins
through the transparent wings of
a red dragonfly

Peeling potatoes —
a hollow at the centre
housed a flying ant

A nest of silence —
when the warbler stopped singing
its tree disappeared
(René Char)

A red dragonfly
floats into the garden room
and floats out again

A wild boar — the pet
of country schoolchildren
sharing their lunch

Ocean bride
  of the winds
    rains children

MORTALITIES

Running to catch up
with the funeral cortège
the dead man's lost dog

The night train's couchette –
so many ghosts of all who
dreamed here one last time

Mingling with the crowds
the shadows of dead soldiers
returning from leave

One black cross rising
above the graveyard wall
in thick-falling snow

The old gardener's
broad thumbnails are wearing deep
mourning bands of black

A dead child's mother
still keeps the retaining seat
buckled behind her

Montparnasse graveyard —
in the gravedigger's hut, two
inflatable dolls

Branded by old age
and the rattan rocking chair
on his naked back

Empty snail shell blown
along a deserted beach
leaving no traces

Under the fresh rouge
a dead woman's lips begin
to move with maggots

Begging
  for life — the insult
    of old age

Candles on crystal
  chandeliers still
    blazing in the grave

Buried alive
  devouring
    his own arm

LALIQUE HAIKU

Dragonflies
   grasshoppers: insects
      by Lalique

Ivy leaves
   enamelled
      by gilt

Hazel catkins
   green enamel on
      translucent horn

Siren diadem —
   three opals
      on branching bronze

Serpent jar —
  chased silver-gilt
    brown-red jasper

Bumblebees
  on flowers — gold,
    glass, enamel

Aquamarine
  set in thistles
    of mauve crystal

Peacock pendant
  enamel, opals,
    loops of gold

LALIQUE TANKA

Dragonfly woman —
chrysoprase breasts — crucified
on wings of moonstone
and diamonds, hovering
syllables transfixed in gold

The Venus slipper
orchid diadem of gold
ivory topaz
on petals of silken shell
cobra-curved one small topaz

FACETS

Monet — old photo —
bearded garden gnome beside
his Giverny bridge

Two small sugar cubes
wrapped in paper printed with
Monet's Giverny

The wine connoisseur's
knowing nod as he sniffs, tastes —
he never complains

The café table —
your right arm, my left arm
in the setting sun

The flower seller
never offers us roses —
our pavement café

It's always raining
every time we say goodbye
it's always raining

I sometimes catch sight
of a face that reminds me
of my dead lover's

By the disused line
the level-crossing keeper's
ivy-smothered house

Thinking I am sad –
finding I am secretly
singing to myself

An immense black cloud –
a flying saucer skimming
just above the roof

I want to see what
the ocean is looking like
when not watching it

A feather floats
  on the water
    of the bird bath

Mirrors welcome
  periods of
    reflection

ZENTSUJI

Santōka — haiku
one step one breath one line rhythm
in summer freedom

To do as I want
and not to do it — this is
what I want to do

Militant living
with implicit vistas in
marriage mirage

In swags of gilt straw
garlanded with chickenshit —
an authentic egg

VISIONS BY SENGAI

Tanka

To grasp their meaning
just by reading the sacred
texts — impossible?
Sweeping dust away with brooms
alone is impossible.

To draw bamboos, one
rule exists, What is that rule?
The Buddha has said:
'To draw without a rule is
the one fundamental rule.'

Han Shan and Shi Te:
sweeping does not clear the dust.
Reading sacred texts
does not allow the reader
to learn how to read letters.

When the east wind blows
the scent of plum blossom wafts
as far as China.
The guardian of plum blossoms
carries a spray in his sleeve.
(on Sugawara no Michizane)

Haiku

Life — a plasterer
on a stepladder, but who
possesses no skill

SYLLOGISMS AFTER CIORAN

Without the promise
of suicide, I'd have killed
myself long ago

I gave God the boot
in order to rid myself
of one old nuisance

Those who have not learned
the joys of being victims
need not try to live

Timidity is
the megalomania of
the misunderstood

But are all my doubts
really doubts? — There is no
more disturbing thought

From the very start
God chose everything for us
— even our neckties

No reason to live —
so why commit suicide?
— no reason to die

Without the good luck
to have had alcoholic
parents, one must drink
oneself to death all life long
to rid oneself of their virtues

To hope
  is to deny
    the future

On his death
  bed he burst
    out laughing

Give unto
  us our
    daily dread

SOME SENRYU

I had the good luck
to grow old without ever
being an adult

As you grow older
you don't care if people see
you picking your nose

A parcel of books
releases the stale smoke of
a shop assistant

Fish-head in waders —
angler caught by his own hook
reeling himself in
(Alberto Savinio)

Telephones sometimes
have a plaintive ring, saying:
"You never call me!"

The unexploded
time bombs laid out on the beach
are six stranded whales

Disintegrating
vapour trails are unzipping
the dawn's empty sky

The public statue
weeping white tears, bird droppings —
scent of lime flowers

A balcony in
the abyss leans and lowers
on a sunset cloud

Hand holding chopsticks
near the top, like compasses
measuring sushi

Hand moves shogi piece —
with middle and forefinger
neatly together

On longdistance trains —
foreign cities announced in
a hometown accent

Tunnel vision at
Waterloo — plastic codfish
swimming in the wind

Ambulance fire engine
police car sirens howling —
today's cathedral bells

The cathedral of
the coaling staithes —
Boulogne-sur-mer!

Cockcrowing squad cars
heehawing ambulances —
New York's fall farmyard

NOT FAREWELL –
JUST AU REVOIR

Eating New Year food —
sushi seaweed paper sticks
to my uvula

Concord's vapour trail
at sunset, brilliant pink
on clear winter skies

Lights of frontier town
still illuminate snow peaks —
mountain flower fields

The sky full of stars —
a nightwatchman's brazier —
smell of bonfire smoke

Heaven is a cool
patch on my burning pillow —
sickroom in summer
(remark by Jean Cocteau
during his final illness)

A door mewing on
its hinges — the cat washing
her newborn kittens

The full moon with eyes
bandaged by a wisp of cloud —
a moth on the pane

The long-limbed swimmers
moving to their starting blocks —
leisurely giraffes

The changing plumage
of the redstart's tail heralds
a change of seasons

Our mother tongue still
is the silence between words —
pauses are meanings